50 Healthy Restaurant Recipes for Home

By: Kelly Johnson

Table of Contents

- Quinoa-Stuffed Bell Peppers
- Grilled Salmon with Avocado Salsa
- Zucchini Noodles with Pesto
- Baked Chicken Breast with Lemon and Herbs
- Spaghetti Squash with Tomato Basil Sauce
- Thai Coconut Curry with Vegetables
- Cauliflower Fried Rice
- Greek Salad with Grilled Chicken
- Black Bean and Sweet Potato Tacos
- Lemon Garlic Shrimp with Asparagus
- Teriyaki Chicken Bowl with Brown Rice
- Veggie-Packed Minestrone Soup
- Roasted Chickpea and Sweet Potato Salad
- Turkey and Spinach Stuffed Mushrooms
- Butternut Squash Soup with Sage
- Grilled Portobello Mushroom Burgers
- Balsamic Glazed Brussels Sprouts
- Roasted Vegetable Quinoa Salad
- Spicy Tuna Poke Bowl
- Baked Eggplant Parmesan
- Lentil and Vegetable Shepherd's Pie
- Cilantro Lime Chicken with Black Beans
- Shrimp and Avocado Lettuce Wraps
- Sweet Potato and Kale Frittata
- Chicken and Vegetable Stir-Fry
- Beet and Goat Cheese Salad
- Healthy Chicken Enchiladas
- Cauliflower and Chickpea Curry
- Grilled Shrimp and Pineapple Skewers
- Stuffed Acorn Squash with Wild Rice
- Spicy Chickpea and Spinach Stew
- Garlic Herb Grilled Chicken

- Mango and Black Bean Salad
- Roasted Red Pepper and Tomato Soup
- Quinoa and Black Bean Burrito Bowls
- Thai Beef Salad
- Lemon Dill Salmon with Roasted Veggies
- Chicken and Avocado Salad
- Lentil and Spinach Soup
- Grilled Veggie and Hummus Wrap
- Mediterranean Quinoa Salad
- Teriyaki Salmon with Broccoli
- Butternut Squash and Black Bean Chili
- Grilled Tofu with Peanut Sauce
- Spinach and Feta Stuffed Chicken
- Sweet Potato Black Bean Burgers
- Roasted Turkey and Veggie Wrap
- Spaghetti Squash Carbonara
- Asian-Inspired Chicken Salad
- Creamy Avocado and Cucumber Soup

Quinoa-Stuffed Bell Peppers

Ingredients:

- 4 large bell peppers (any color)
- 1 cup quinoa, rinsed
- 2 cups vegetable or chicken broth
- 1 tablespoon olive oil
- 1 small onion, finely chopped
- 2 cloves garlic, minced
- 1 cup black beans, drained and rinsed
- 1 cup corn kernels (fresh, frozen, or canned)
- 1 cup diced tomatoes
- 1 teaspoon ground cumin
- 1 teaspoon smoked paprika
- Salt and pepper to taste
- 1/2 cup shredded cheese (optional)
- Fresh cilantro, chopped (for garnish)

Instructions:

1. **Preheat Oven**: Preheat your oven to 375°F (190°C).
2. **Cook Quinoa**: In a medium saucepan, combine the quinoa and broth. Bring to a boil, then reduce heat to low, cover, and simmer for about 15 minutes, or until the quinoa is cooked and the liquid is absorbed. Fluff with a fork.
3. **Prepare Peppers**: Cut the tops off the bell peppers and remove the seeds and membranes. Lightly brush the peppers with olive oil and place them in a baking dish.
4. **Cook Filling**: Heat olive oil in a skillet over medium heat. Add the chopped onion and cook until translucent, about 3-4 minutes. Add the garlic and cook for an additional 1 minute.
5. **Combine Ingredients**: Stir in the black beans, corn, diced tomatoes, cumin, smoked paprika, salt, and pepper. Cook for about 2 minutes, until the mixture is heated through.
6. **Mix Quinoa**: Add the cooked quinoa to the skillet and mix everything together. Cook for another 2 minutes, allowing the flavors to meld.
7. **Stuff Peppers**: Spoon the quinoa mixture into the prepared bell peppers, packing the filling tightly. If using cheese, sprinkle it on top.
8. **Bake**: Cover the baking dish with foil and bake for 30 minutes. Remove the foil and bake for an additional 10 minutes, or until the peppers are tender and the cheese is melted and bubbly.
9. **Garnish and Serve**: Remove from the oven and let cool slightly. Garnish with chopped cilantro before serving.

Enjoy your healthy and flavorful Quinoa-Stuffed Bell Peppers!

Grilled Salmon with Avocado Salsa

Ingredients:

- **For the Salmon:**
    - 4 salmon fillets
    - 2 tablespoons olive oil
    - 1 lemon, juiced
    - 2 cloves garlic, minced
    - 1 teaspoon dried oregano
    - Salt and pepper to taste
- **For the Avocado Salsa:**
    - 2 ripe avocados, diced
    - 1 cup cherry tomatoes, halved
    - 1/4 cup red onion, finely chopped
    - 1 jalapeño, seeded and minced (optional)
    - 2 tablespoons fresh cilantro, chopped
    - Juice of 1 lime
    - Salt to taste

Instructions:

1. **Marinate Salmon**: In a small bowl, mix olive oil, lemon juice, minced garlic, dried oregano, salt, and pepper. Brush the mixture over the salmon fillets and let them marinate for 15-20 minutes.
2. **Prepare Grill**: Preheat your grill to medium-high heat. Oil the grill grates to prevent sticking.
3. **Grill Salmon**: Place the salmon fillets on the grill skin-side down. Grill for 4-6 minutes per side, or until the salmon is cooked through and flakes easily with a fork.
4. **Make Salsa**: While the salmon is grilling, combine avocados, cherry tomatoes, red onion, jalapeño, cilantro, lime juice, and salt in a bowl. Gently toss to combine.
5. **Serve**: Remove the salmon from the grill and serve with a generous topping of avocado salsa.

Enjoy your fresh and vibrant Grilled Salmon with Avocado Salsa!

Zucchini Noodles with Pesto

Ingredients:

- 4 medium zucchinis
- 1/4 cup olive oil
- Salt and pepper to taste
- **For the Pesto:**
    - 1 cup fresh basil leaves
    - 1/2 cup pine nuts (or walnuts)
    - 1/2 cup grated Parmesan cheese
    - 2 cloves garlic
    - 1/2 cup olive oil
    - Salt and pepper to taste

Instructions:

1. **Prepare Zucchini Noodles**: Using a spiralizer, create noodles from the zucchinis. If you don't have a spiralizer, you can use a julienne peeler or a mandoline.
2. **Cook Noodles**: Heat olive oil in a large skillet over medium heat. Add the zucchini noodles and cook for 2-3 minutes, stirring occasionally, until they are tender but still al dente. Season with salt and pepper. Remove from heat.
3. **Make Pesto**: In a food processor, combine basil, pine nuts, Parmesan cheese, and garlic. Pulse until finely chopped. With the processor running, gradually add olive oil until the mixture is smooth. Season with salt and pepper.
4. **Combine**: Toss the cooked zucchini noodles with the pesto until evenly coated.
5. **Serve**: Serve immediately, garnished with extra Parmesan if desired.

Enjoy your fresh and flavorful Zucchini Noodles with Pesto!

Baked Chicken Breast with Lemon and Herbs

Ingredients:

- 4 boneless, skinless chicken breasts
- 2 tablespoons olive oil
- Juice of 1 lemon
- 2 cloves garlic, minced
- 1 tablespoon fresh thyme leaves (or 1 teaspoon dried thyme)
- 1 tablespoon fresh rosemary, chopped (or 1 teaspoon dried rosemary)
- Salt and pepper to taste
- Lemon slices for garnish (optional)

Instructions:

1. **Preheat Oven**: Preheat your oven to 375°F (190°C).
2. **Prepare Chicken**: Place chicken breasts in a baking dish. Drizzle with olive oil and lemon juice. Rub the minced garlic, thyme, rosemary, salt, and pepper all over the chicken breasts.
3. **Bake**: Bake for 25-30 minutes, or until the chicken reaches an internal temperature of 165°F (74°C) and is cooked through.
4. **Rest and Serve**: Let the chicken rest for 5 minutes before slicing. Garnish with lemon slices if desired.

Enjoy your flavorful and juicy Baked Chicken Breast with Lemon and Herbs!

Spaghetti Squash with Tomato Basil Sauce

Ingredients:

- 1 large spaghetti squash
- 2 tablespoons olive oil
- Salt and pepper to taste
- **For the Tomato Basil Sauce:**
    - 1 tablespoon olive oil
    - 1 onion, finely chopped
    - 2 cloves garlic, minced
    - 1 can (14.5 oz) diced tomatoes
    - 1/4 cup tomato paste
    - 1 teaspoon dried oregano
    - 1 teaspoon dried basil
    - Salt and pepper to taste
    - 1/4 cup fresh basil, chopped

Instructions:

1. **Prepare Spaghetti Squash**: Preheat your oven to 400°F (200°C). Cut the spaghetti squash in half lengthwise and remove the seeds. Drizzle with olive oil, season with salt and pepper, and place cut-side down on a baking sheet. Bake for 40-45 minutes, or until tender.
2. **Make Sauce**: While the squash bakes, heat olive oil in a saucepan over medium heat. Add onion and cook until translucent, about 5 minutes. Stir in garlic and cook for 1 minute. Add diced tomatoes, tomato paste, oregano, basil, salt, and pepper. Simmer for 10-15 minutes. Stir in fresh basil just before serving.
3. **Scrape Squash**: Once the squash is done, let it cool slightly. Use a fork to scrape the flesh into strands.
4. **Combine and Serve**: Top the spaghetti squash with the tomato basil sauce and serve.

Enjoy your light and delicious Spaghetti Squash with Tomato Basil Sauce!

Thai Coconut Curry with Vegetables

Ingredients:

- 1 tablespoon coconut oil
- 1 onion, chopped
- 2 cloves garlic, minced
- 1 tablespoon fresh ginger, minced
- 2 tablespoons red curry paste
- 1 can (14 oz) coconut milk
- 1 cup vegetable broth
- 2 tablespoons fish sauce (or soy sauce for a vegetarian version)
- 1 tablespoon brown sugar (or coconut sugar)
- 1 cup carrots, sliced
- 1 red bell pepper, sliced
- 1 cup snap peas
- 1 cup broccoli florets
- 1 cup baby corn (optional)
- 1 lime, juiced
- Fresh cilantro, chopped (for garnish)
- Cooked jasmine rice or rice noodles (for serving)

Instructions:

1. **Sauté Aromatics**: Heat coconut oil in a large skillet or wok over medium heat. Add onion and cook until translucent, about 5 minutes. Stir in garlic and ginger and cook for another minute.
2. **Add Curry Paste**: Add red curry paste and cook for 1-2 minutes, stirring frequently, until fragrant.
3. **Make Sauce**: Pour in the coconut milk and vegetable broth. Stir in fish sauce and brown sugar. Bring to a simmer.
4. **Cook Vegetables**: Add carrots, bell pepper, snap peas, broccoli, and baby corn. Simmer for 5-7 minutes, or until vegetables are tender-crisp.
5. **Finish and Serve**: Stir in lime juice and adjust seasoning with more fish sauce or salt if needed. Serve over cooked jasmine rice or rice noodles. Garnish with fresh cilantro.

Enjoy your flavorful and creamy Thai Coconut Curry with Vegetables!

Cauliflower Fried Rice

Ingredients:

- 1 large head of cauliflower, grated or processed into rice-sized pieces
- 2 tablespoons sesame oil
- 2 cloves garlic, minced
- 1 small onion, diced
- 1 cup mixed vegetables (carrots, peas, corn)
- 2 eggs, beaten
- 2 green onions, sliced
- 3 tablespoons low-sodium soy sauce
- Salt and pepper to taste
- Optional: cooked chicken, shrimp, or tofu for added protein

Instructions:

1. **Prepare Cauliflower**: Grate or process the cauliflower until it resembles rice grains.
2. **Cook Aromatics**: Heat sesame oil in a large skillet or wok over medium-high heat. Add garlic and onion, cooking until fragrant and translucent, about 3-4 minutes.
3. **Add Vegetables**: Stir in the mixed vegetables and cook for another 3-4 minutes until tender.
4. **Cook Eggs**: Push the vegetables to one side of the skillet and pour the beaten eggs into the empty side. Scramble and cook until just set, then mix with the vegetables.
5. **Add Cauliflower**: Add the cauliflower rice and soy sauce to the skillet. Stir well and cook for 5-7 minutes, or until the cauliflower is tender and slightly crispy. Season with salt and pepper.
6. **Finish**: Stir in green onions and optional protein if using. Cook for an additional 1-2 minutes.

Enjoy your healthy and delicious Cauliflower Fried Rice!

Greek Salad with Grilled Chicken

Ingredients:

- **For the Salad:**
    - 4 cups mixed greens (e.g., romaine, spinach)
    - 1 cup cherry tomatoes, halved
    - 1 cucumber, sliced
    - 1/2 red onion, thinly sliced
    - 1/2 cup Kalamata olives
    - 1/2 cup feta cheese, crumbled
- **For the Grilled Chicken:**
    - 2 boneless, skinless chicken breasts
    - 2 tablespoons olive oil
    - Juice of 1 lemon
    - 1 teaspoon dried oregano
    - Salt and pepper to taste
- **For the Dressing:**
    - 1/4 cup olive oil
    - 2 tablespoons red wine vinegar
    - 1 teaspoon dried oregano
    - 1 garlic clove, minced
    - Salt and pepper to taste

Instructions:

1. **Marinate Chicken**: In a bowl, mix olive oil, lemon juice, oregano, salt, and pepper. Marinate the chicken breasts for at least 20 minutes.
2. **Grill Chicken**: Preheat the grill to medium-high heat. Grill chicken breasts for 6-8 minutes per side, or until cooked through. Let rest for 5 minutes before slicing.
3. **Prepare Salad**: In a large bowl, combine mixed greens, cherry tomatoes, cucumber, red onion, olives, and feta cheese.
4. **Make Dressing**: Whisk together olive oil, red wine vinegar, oregano, garlic, salt, and pepper in a small bowl.
5. **Assemble**: Slice the grilled chicken and place it on top of the salad. Drizzle with the dressing and toss gently.

Enjoy your refreshing Greek Salad with Grilled Chicken!

Black Bean and Sweet Potato Tacos

Ingredients:

- 1 large sweet potato, peeled and diced
- 1 tablespoon olive oil
- 1 teaspoon ground cumin
- 1 teaspoon smoked paprika
- 1/2 teaspoon chili powder
- Salt and pepper to taste
- 1 can (15 oz) black beans, drained and rinsed
- 1/2 cup red onion, finely chopped
- 1 cup corn kernels (fresh, frozen, or canned)
- 1/4 cup fresh cilantro, chopped
- 8 small tortillas (corn or flour)
- Optional toppings: avocado slices, salsa, sour cream, shredded cheese, lime wedges

Instructions:

1. **Roast Sweet Potatoes**: Preheat your oven to 400°F (200°C). Toss diced sweet potatoes with olive oil, cumin, smoked paprika, chili powder, salt, and pepper. Spread in a single layer on a baking sheet. Roast for 25-30 minutes, or until tender and slightly caramelized, stirring halfway through.
2. **Prepare Filling**: While the sweet potatoes are roasting, heat a skillet over medium heat. Add a splash of olive oil, then sauté the red onion until softened, about 5 minutes. Add the black beans and corn, and cook for an additional 2-3 minutes until heated through. Stir in the fresh cilantro.
3. **Warm Tortillas**: Heat tortillas in a dry skillet over medium heat for about 30 seconds per side, or until warm and pliable.
4. **Assemble Tacos**: Fill each tortilla with a portion of the roasted sweet potatoes and the black bean-corn mixture. Add optional toppings like avocado, salsa, sour cream, shredded cheese, or a squeeze of lime.
5. **Serve**: Serve immediately and enjoy!

These Black Bean and Sweet Potato Tacos are nutritious and full of flavor!

Lemon Garlic Shrimp with Asparagus

Ingredients:

- 1 lb (450 g) large shrimp, peeled and deveined
- 1 bunch asparagus, trimmed and cut into 2-inch pieces
- 2 tablespoons olive oil
- 4 cloves garlic, minced
- Juice of 1 lemon
- Zest of 1 lemon
- 1/4 teaspoon red pepper flakes (optional)
- 1/4 cup fresh parsley, chopped
- Salt and pepper to taste
- Lemon wedges for serving (optional)

Instructions:

1. **Prepare Asparagus**: Preheat your oven to 400°F (200°C). Toss the asparagus pieces with 1 tablespoon of olive oil, salt, and pepper. Spread them out on a baking sheet in a single layer.
2. **Roast Asparagus**: Roast asparagus in the preheated oven for 10-12 minutes, or until tender and slightly crisped. Remove from the oven and set aside.
3. **Cook Shrimp**: While the asparagus is roasting, heat 1 tablespoon of olive oil in a large skillet over medium-high heat. Add the minced garlic and cook for about 1 minute, until fragrant.
4. **Add Shrimp**: Add the shrimp to the skillet, seasoning with salt, pepper, and red pepper flakes (if using). Cook for 2-3 minutes per side, or until the shrimp are pink and opaque.
5. **Combine and Finish**: Once the shrimp are cooked, add the roasted asparagus to the skillet. Stir in the lemon juice and lemon zest. Cook for another 1-2 minutes, until everything is heated through and well combined.
6. **Garnish and Serve**: Remove from heat and stir in the chopped parsley. Serve immediately with lemon wedges if desired.

Enjoy your flavorful and light Lemon Garlic Shrimp with Asparagus!

Teriyaki Chicken Bowl with Brown Rice

Ingredients:

- **For the Teriyaki Chicken:**
    - 1 lb (450 g) boneless, skinless chicken thighs or breasts
    - 1/4 cup low-sodium soy sauce
    - 2 tablespoons honey or maple syrup
    - 2 tablespoons rice vinegar
    - 1 tablespoon sesame oil
    - 2 cloves garlic, minced
    - 1 teaspoon freshly grated ginger
    - 1 tablespoon cornstarch mixed with 2 tablespoons water (optional, for thickening)
- **For the Brown Rice:**
    - 1 cup brown rice
    - 2 cups water or chicken broth
- **For the Bowl:**
    - 1 cup broccoli florets
    - 1 cup shredded carrots
    - 1/2 cup snap peas
    - 1/4 cup sliced green onions
    - 1 tablespoon sesame seeds (optional)
    - Fresh cilantro for garnish (optional)

Instructions:

1. **Cook Brown Rice**: In a medium saucepan, bring 2 cups of water or chicken broth to a boil. Add the brown rice, reduce heat to low, cover, and simmer for 40-45 minutes, or until the rice is tender and the liquid is absorbed. Fluff with a fork and set aside.
2. **Prepare Teriyaki Sauce**: In a small bowl, whisk together soy sauce, honey or maple syrup, rice vinegar, sesame oil, minced garlic, and grated ginger. Set aside.
3. **Cook Chicken**: Heat a large skillet or grill pan over medium-high heat. Add a splash of oil if needed. Cook the chicken for 5-7 minutes per side, or until fully cooked and the internal temperature reaches 165°F (74°C). Remove from the pan and let rest for a few minutes before slicing.
4. **Thicken Sauce (Optional)**: While the chicken is resting, pour the teriyaki sauce into the skillet used for the chicken. Bring to a simmer and add the cornstarch mixture if using. Cook for 1-2 minutes until the sauce thickens slightly.
5. **Cook Vegetables**: Steam or sauté the broccoli, carrots, and snap peas until tender-crisp, about 3-5 minutes.
6. **Assemble Bowls**: Divide the cooked brown rice among bowls. Top with sliced chicken, vegetables, and a drizzle of teriyaki sauce. Garnish with green onions, sesame seeds, and fresh cilantro if desired.

7. **Serve**: Serve immediately and enjoy your delicious Teriyaki Chicken Bowl with Brown Rice!

Veggie-Packed Minestrone Soup

Ingredients:

- 2 tablespoons olive oil
- 1 onion, diced
- 2 cloves garlic, minced
- 2 carrots, diced
- 2 celery stalks, diced
- 1 zucchini, diced
- 1 red bell pepper, diced
- 1 cup green beans, chopped
- 1 can (14.5 oz) diced tomatoes
- 4 cups vegetable broth
- 1 cup cooked pasta or small pasta shapes (like orzo or elbow macaroni)
- 1 can (15 oz) kidney beans, drained and rinsed
- 1 cup spinach or kale, chopped
- 1 teaspoon dried oregano
- 1 teaspoon dried basil
- Salt and pepper to taste
- Grated Parmesan cheese for serving (optional)

Instructions:

1. **Sauté Vegetables**: Heat olive oil in a large pot over medium heat. Add onion, garlic, carrots, and celery. Cook until vegetables are softened, about 5-7 minutes.
2. **Add Remaining Vegetables**: Stir in zucchini, red bell pepper, and green beans. Cook for another 3-4 minutes.
3. **Add Liquids and Seasoning**: Pour in diced tomatoes and vegetable broth. Stir in oregano and basil. Bring to a boil, then reduce heat and simmer for 10-15 minutes, until vegetables are tender.
4. **Add Beans and Pasta**: Stir in cooked pasta and kidney beans. Simmer for another 5 minutes, until heated through.
5. **Finish with Greens**: Add spinach or kale and cook for an additional 2-3 minutes, until wilted.
6. **Season and Serve**: Season with salt and pepper to taste. Serve hot, topped with grated Parmesan cheese if desired.

Enjoy your hearty and nutritious Veggie-Packed Minestrone Soup!

Roasted Chickpea and Sweet Potato Salad

Ingredients:

- **For the Roasted Chickpeas and Sweet Potatoes:**
    - 1 can (15 oz) chickpeas, drained and rinsed
    - 2 medium sweet potatoes, peeled and diced
    - 2 tablespoons olive oil
    - 1 teaspoon smoked paprika
    - 1/2 teaspoon ground cumin
    - 1/2 teaspoon garlic powder
    - Salt and pepper to taste
- **For the Salad:**
    - 4 cups mixed greens (e.g., spinach, arugula)
    - 1/4 red onion, thinly sliced
    - 1/4 cup crumbled feta cheese (optional)
    - 1/4 cup chopped fresh parsley
- **For the Dressing:**
    - 3 tablespoons olive oil
    - 2 tablespoons balsamic vinegar
    - 1 teaspoon Dijon mustard
    - 1 teaspoon honey or maple syrup
    - Salt and pepper to taste

Instructions:

1. **Preheat Oven**: Preheat your oven to 400°F (200°C).
2. **Roast Chickpeas and Sweet Potatoes**: Toss the chickpeas and sweet potato cubes with olive oil, smoked paprika, cumin, garlic powder, salt, and pepper. Spread them on a baking sheet in a single layer. Roast for 25-30 minutes, or until the sweet potatoes are tender and the chickpeas are crispy, stirring halfway through.
3. **Prepare Salad**: In a large bowl, combine mixed greens, red onion, feta cheese (if using), and chopped parsley.
4. **Make Dressing**: Whisk together olive oil, balsamic vinegar, Dijon mustard, honey, salt, and pepper in a small bowl.
5. **Assemble Salad**: Once the chickpeas and sweet potatoes are roasted and slightly cooled, add them to the salad. Drizzle with dressing and toss gently.
6. **Serve**: Serve immediately or refrigerate until ready to eat.

Enjoy your hearty and flavorful Roasted Chickpea and Sweet Potato Salad!

Turkey and Spinach Stuffed Mushrooms

Ingredients:

- 12 large button or cremini mushrooms
- 1 tablespoon olive oil
- 1/2 pound ground turkey
- 2 cloves garlic, minced
- 1 small onion, finely chopped
- 1 cup fresh spinach, chopped
- 1/4 cup grated Parmesan cheese
- 1/4 cup breadcrumbs (or almond flour for a gluten-free option)
- 1/4 teaspoon dried thyme
- 1/4 teaspoon dried oregano
- Salt and pepper to taste
- Fresh parsley, chopped (for garnish)

Instructions:

1. **Preheat Oven**: Preheat your oven to 375°F (190°C).
2. **Prepare Mushrooms**: Clean the mushrooms and remove the stems. Set the mushroom caps aside. Finely chop the stems and reserve for the filling.
3. **Cook Filling**: Heat olive oil in a skillet over medium heat. Add the ground turkey, garlic, and onion. Cook until the turkey is browned and cooked through, breaking it up with a spoon, about 5-7 minutes.
4. **Add Vegetables**: Stir in the chopped mushroom stems and cook for another 2-3 minutes. Add the chopped spinach and cook until wilted, about 1-2 minutes. Remove from heat and stir in Parmesan cheese, breadcrumbs, thyme, oregano, salt, and pepper.
5. **Stuff Mushrooms**: Place the mushroom caps on a baking sheet. Spoon the turkey and spinach mixture into each mushroom cap, packing it slightly.
6. **Bake**: Bake in the preheated oven for 20-25 minutes, or until the mushrooms are tender and the filling is golden brown.
7. **Garnish and Serve**: Garnish with chopped fresh parsley before serving.

Enjoy your flavorful and nutritious Turkey and Spinach Stuffed Mushrooms!

Butternut Squash Soup with Sage

Ingredients:

- 1 large butternut squash, peeled, seeded, and cubed
- 2 tablespoons olive oil
- 1 onion, chopped
- 2 cloves garlic, minced
- 1 teaspoon fresh sage, chopped (or 1/2 teaspoon dried sage)
- 4 cups vegetable or chicken broth
- 1/2 cup coconut milk or heavy cream (optional, for creaminess)
- Salt and pepper to taste
- Fresh sage leaves for garnish (optional)

Instructions:

1. **Prepare Squash**: Preheat your oven to 400°F (200°C). Toss butternut squash cubes with 1 tablespoon of olive oil, salt, and pepper. Spread on a baking sheet and roast for 25-30 minutes, or until tender and caramelized.
2. **Cook Aromatics**: While the squash roasts, heat the remaining olive oil in a large pot over medium heat. Add the chopped onion and cook until softened, about 5 minutes. Stir in garlic and sage, and cook for another 1-2 minutes until fragrant.
3. **Combine Ingredients**: Once the squash is roasted, add it to the pot with the onions and garlic. Pour in the broth and bring to a simmer. Cook for 10 minutes to let the flavors meld.
4. **Blend Soup**: Use an immersion blender to puree the soup until smooth. Alternatively, transfer the soup in batches to a blender and blend until smooth.
5. **Finish and Serve**: Stir in coconut milk or heavy cream if using, and adjust seasoning with salt and pepper. Garnish with fresh sage leaves if desired.

Enjoy your creamy and aromatic Butternut Squash Soup with Sage!

Grilled Portobello Mushroom Burgers

Ingredients:

- 4 large portobello mushrooms, stems removed
- 1/4 cup balsamic vinegar
- 1/4 cup olive oil
- 2 cloves garlic, minced
- 1 tablespoon soy sauce or tamari
- 1 teaspoon dried oregano
- Salt and pepper to taste
- 4 burger buns
- Toppings: lettuce, tomato slices, red onion, avocado, cheese (optional)

Instructions:

1. **Marinate Mushrooms**: In a bowl, whisk together balsamic vinegar, olive oil, minced garlic, soy sauce, oregano, salt, and pepper. Add the portobello mushrooms and let them marinate for at least 15 minutes.
2. **Preheat Grill**: Preheat your grill to medium-high heat.
3. **Grill Mushrooms**: Place the marinated mushrooms on the grill, gill side down. Grill for 5-7 minutes per side, or until tender and slightly charred.
4. **Prepare Buns**: During the last 2 minutes of grilling, place the burger buns on the grill to toast lightly.
5. **Assemble Burgers**: Place each grilled mushroom cap on a bun. Top with your favorite burger toppings such as lettuce, tomato, red onion, avocado, and cheese if desired.
6. **Serve**: Serve immediately and enjoy your flavorful Grilled Portobello Mushroom Burgers!

Balsamic Glazed Brussels Sprouts

Ingredients:

- 1 lb (450 g) Brussels sprouts, trimmed and halved
- 2 tablespoons olive oil
- Salt and pepper to taste
- 1/4 cup balsamic vinegar
- 2 tablespoons honey or maple syrup
- 2 tablespoons grated Parmesan cheese (optional)
- Fresh parsley, chopped (for garnish, optional)

Instructions:

1. **Preheat Oven**: Preheat your oven to 425°F (220°C).
2. **Prepare Brussels Sprouts**: Toss Brussels sprouts with olive oil, salt, and pepper. Spread them in a single layer on a baking sheet.
3. **Roast**: Roast in the preheated oven for 20-25 minutes, or until the Brussels sprouts are tender and caramelized, stirring halfway through.
4. **Make Balsamic Glaze**: While the Brussels sprouts roast, combine balsamic vinegar and honey (or maple syrup) in a small saucepan. Simmer over medium heat until reduced by half and slightly thickened, about 5-7 minutes. Remove from heat.
5. **Glaze and Serve**: Drizzle the balsamic glaze over the roasted Brussels sprouts. Toss to coat. Sprinkle with Parmesan cheese and fresh parsley if desired.
6. **Serve**: Enjoy your sweet and tangy Balsamic Glazed Brussels Sprouts!

Roasted Vegetable Quinoa Salad

Ingredients:

- **For the Salad:**
    - 1 cup quinoa, rinsed
    - 2 cups water or vegetable broth
    - 1 red bell pepper, diced
    - 1 yellow bell pepper, diced
    - 1 medium zucchini, diced
    - 1 cup cherry tomatoes, halved
    - 1/2 red onion, diced
    - 2 tablespoons olive oil
    - Salt and pepper to taste
    - 1/4 cup fresh basil, chopped (or parsley)
    - 1/4 cup feta cheese, crumbled (optional)
    - 1/4 cup pine nuts or chopped walnuts (optional)
- **For the Dressing:**
    - 1/4 cup olive oil
    - 2 tablespoons balsamic vinegar
    - 1 tablespoon Dijon mustard
    - 1 clove garlic, minced
    - 1 teaspoon honey or maple syrup
    - Salt and pepper to taste

Instructions:

1. **Cook Quinoa**: In a medium saucepan, bring 2 cups of water or vegetable broth to a boil. Add quinoa, reduce heat to low, cover, and simmer for 15 minutes, or until quinoa is tender and liquid is absorbed. Fluff with a fork and let cool.
2. **Prepare Vegetables**: Preheat your oven to 425°F (220°C). Toss red bell pepper, yellow bell pepper, zucchini, cherry tomatoes, and red onion with olive oil, salt, and pepper. Spread on a baking sheet in a single layer.
3. **Roast Vegetables**: Roast in the preheated oven for 20-25 minutes, or until vegetables are tender and slightly caramelized, stirring halfway through. Let cool slightly.
4. **Make Dressing**: In a small bowl, whisk together olive oil, balsamic vinegar, Dijon mustard, minced garlic, honey or maple syrup, salt, and pepper.
5. **Combine Salad**: In a large bowl, combine cooked quinoa, roasted vegetables, and fresh basil. Drizzle with dressing and toss to coat.
6. **Add Toppings**: If desired, sprinkle with feta cheese and pine nuts or walnuts.
7. **Serve**: Serve the salad at room temperature or chilled.

Enjoy your vibrant and nutritious Roasted Vegetable Quinoa Salad!

Spicy Tuna Poke Bowl

Ingredients:

- **For the Poke Bowl:**
    - 1 lb (450 g) sushi-grade tuna, diced
    - 2 tablespoons soy sauce
    - 1 tablespoon sesame oil
    - 1 tablespoon Sriracha or other hot sauce (adjust to taste)
    - 1 teaspoon honey or maple syrup
    - 1 avocado, sliced
    - 1 cup cooked sushi rice or brown rice
    - 1 cup edamame, cooked
    - 1 cup cucumber, thinly sliced
    - 1/2 cup shredded carrots
    - 1/4 cup pickled ginger (optional)
    - 2 tablespoons sliced green onions
    - 1 tablespoon sesame seeds
    - Seaweed salad (optional, for garnish)
- **For the Sauce:**
    - 2 tablespoons soy sauce
    - 1 tablespoon rice vinegar
    - 1 teaspoon sesame oil
    - 1 teaspoon honey or maple syrup

Instructions:

1. **Prepare Tuna**: In a bowl, mix diced tuna with soy sauce, sesame oil, Sriracha, and honey. Let marinate in the refrigerator for 10-15 minutes.
2. **Cook Rice**: Cook sushi rice according to package instructions. Let it cool slightly.
3. **Prepare Sauce**: In a small bowl, whisk together soy sauce, rice vinegar, sesame oil, and honey.
4. **Assemble Bowls**: Divide the cooked rice among bowls. Top with marinated tuna, avocado slices, edamame, cucumber, shredded carrots, and pickled ginger if using.
5. **Garnish**: Drizzle with the prepared sauce. Sprinkle with sliced green onions, sesame seeds, and seaweed salad if desired.
6. **Serve**: Serve immediately and enjoy your fresh and spicy Tuna Poke Bowl!

Baked Eggplant Parmesan

Ingredients:

- **For the Eggplant:**
    - 2 medium eggplants, sliced into 1/4-inch rounds
    - Salt (for sweating the eggplant)
    - 1 cup all-purpose flour (or gluten-free flour)
    - 2 large eggs
    - 1 cup breadcrumbs (or gluten-free breadcrumbs)
    - 1/2 cup grated Parmesan cheese
    - 1 teaspoon dried oregano
    - 1 teaspoon dried basil
    - 1/2 teaspoon garlic powder
    - Olive oil spray or 2 tablespoons olive oil
- **For the Sauce:**
    - 2 cups marinara sauce (store-bought or homemade)
    - 1/2 cup fresh basil, chopped (optional, for added flavor)
- **For the Topping:**
    - 1 1/2 cups shredded mozzarella cheese
    - 1/4 cup grated Parmesan cheese

Instructions:

1. **Preheat Oven**: Preheat your oven to 375°F (190°C).
2. **Prepare Eggplant**: Sprinkle eggplant slices with salt and place them on a paper towel or a rack. Let them sit for 20 minutes to draw out excess moisture and bitterness. Rinse the salt off and pat the slices dry with paper towels.
3. **Bread the Eggplant**:
    - Set up a breading station: Place flour in one bowl, beat eggs in another bowl, and mix breadcrumbs, Parmesan cheese, oregano, basil, and garlic powder in a third bowl.
    - Dredge each eggplant slice in flour, then dip in beaten eggs, and coat with the breadcrumb mixture.
4. **Bake Eggplant**: Arrange the breaded eggplant slices in a single layer on a baking sheet lined with parchment paper. Lightly spray or brush with olive oil. Bake for 25-30 minutes, flipping halfway through, until golden brown and crispy.
5. **Assemble the Dish**:
    - Spread a thin layer of marinara sauce in the bottom of a baking dish.
    - Layer half of the baked eggplant slices on top of the sauce.
    - Spoon more marinara sauce over the eggplant and sprinkle with half of the shredded mozzarella cheese.

- Add the remaining eggplant slices, more marinara sauce, and top with the remaining mozzarella cheese and Parmesan cheese.
6. **Bake Again**: Bake in the preheated oven for 20-25 minutes, or until the cheese is melted and bubbly. If desired, broil for 1-2 minutes to get a golden-brown top.
7. **Garnish and Serve**: Garnish with fresh basil if desired. Let it cool slightly before serving.

Enjoy your delicious and comforting Baked Eggplant Parmesan!

Lentil and Vegetable Shepherd's Pie

Ingredients:

- **For the Filling:**
    - 1 tablespoon olive oil
    - 1 onion, diced
    - 2 cloves garlic, minced
    - 2 carrots, diced
    - 2 celery stalks, diced
    - 1 cup mushrooms, diced
    - 1 cup cooked lentils (green or brown)
    - 1 cup vegetable broth
    - 1 tablespoon tomato paste
    - 1 teaspoon dried thyme
    - 1 teaspoon dried rosemary
    - Salt and pepper to taste
    - 1 cup frozen peas
- **For the Mashed Potatoes:**
    - 4 large potatoes, peeled and cubed
    - 2 tablespoons butter or vegan alternative
    - 1/4 cup milk or plant-based milk
    - Salt and pepper to taste

Instructions:

1. **Prepare Mashed Potatoes**:
    - Boil the potatoes in a large pot of salted water until tender, about 15-20 minutes. Drain and return to the pot.
    - Add butter and milk to the potatoes. Mash until smooth and creamy. Season with salt and pepper. Set aside.
2. **Prepare Filling**:
    - Heat olive oil in a large skillet over medium heat. Add onion and garlic, and cook until softened, about 5 minutes.
    - Stir in carrots, celery, and mushrooms. Cook for an additional 5-7 minutes until vegetables are tender.
    - Add cooked lentils, vegetable broth, tomato paste, thyme, rosemary, salt, and pepper. Simmer for 10 minutes, until the mixture thickens slightly.
    - Stir in frozen peas and cook for another 2 minutes. Remove from heat.
3. **Assemble Pie**:
    - Preheat your oven to 400°F (200°C).
    - Spread the lentil and vegetable filling evenly in the bottom of a baking dish.

        - Spoon the mashed potatoes over the filling, spreading them out evenly and smoothing the top with a spatula.
 4. **Bake**:
        - Bake in the preheated oven for 20-25 minutes, or until the top is lightly golden and the filling is bubbling.
 5. **Serve**:
        - Let the pie cool for a few minutes before serving.

Enjoy your hearty and comforting Lentil and Vegetable Shepherd's Pie!

Cilantro Lime Chicken with Black Beans

Ingredients:

- **For the Chicken:**
    - 1 lb (450 g) boneless, skinless chicken breasts or thighs
    - 2 tablespoons olive oil
    - Juice of 2 limes
    - 1/4 cup fresh cilantro, chopped
    - 3 cloves garlic, minced
    - 1 teaspoon ground cumin
    - 1/2 teaspoon paprika
    - Salt and pepper to taste
- **For the Black Beans:**
    - 1 can (15 oz) black beans, drained and rinsed
    - 1/2 cup red bell pepper, diced
    - 1/2 cup corn kernels (fresh, frozen, or canned)
    - 1/2 teaspoon ground cumin
    - 1/4 teaspoon chili powder
    - Salt and pepper to taste
    - 1 tablespoon fresh cilantro, chopped (optional)

Instructions:

1. **Marinate Chicken**:
    - In a bowl, mix olive oil, lime juice, chopped cilantro, garlic, cumin, paprika, salt, and pepper.
    - Add the chicken breasts or thighs and coat well. Let marinate for at least 30 minutes, or up to 2 hours in the refrigerator.
2. **Cook Chicken**:
    - Heat a grill or skillet over medium-high heat. Cook the chicken for 5-7 minutes per side, or until fully cooked and the internal temperature reaches 165°F (74°C). Let rest for a few minutes before slicing.
3. **Prepare Black Beans**:
    - In a medium saucepan, combine black beans, red bell pepper, corn, cumin, chili powder, salt, and pepper. Heat over medium heat until warmed through, about 5 minutes. Stir in fresh cilantro if using.
4. **Serve**:
    - Slice the cooked chicken and serve over the black bean mixture or alongside it.

Enjoy your flavorful and fresh Cilantro Lime Chicken with Black Beans!

Shrimp and Avocado Lettuce Wraps

Ingredients:

- **For the Shrimp:**
    - 1 lb (450 g) large shrimp, peeled and deveined
    - 2 tablespoons olive oil
    - 2 cloves garlic, minced
    - 1 teaspoon smoked paprika
    - 1/2 teaspoon ground cumin
    - 1/4 teaspoon red pepper flakes (optional, for heat)
    - Salt and pepper to taste
- **For the Wraps:**
    - 1 head of Romaine lettuce or Butter lettuce (leaves separated and washed)
    - 1 avocado, diced
    - 1/2 cup cherry tomatoes, halved
    - 1/4 cup red onion, thinly sliced
    - 1/4 cup fresh cilantro, chopped
    - Lime wedges for serving
- **For the Dressing (Optional):**
    - 2 tablespoons Greek yogurt or sour cream
    - 1 tablespoon lime juice
    - 1 teaspoon honey or maple syrup
    - Salt and pepper to taste

Instructions:

1. **Cook the Shrimp:**
    - In a large bowl, toss the shrimp with olive oil, garlic, smoked paprika, cumin, red pepper flakes, salt, and pepper.
    - Heat a skillet over medium-high heat. Cook the shrimp for 2-3 minutes per side, or until pink and opaque. Remove from heat and set aside.
2. **Prepare the Lettuce Wraps:**
    - Arrange the lettuce leaves on a serving platter.
    - In a small bowl, gently toss together the diced avocado, cherry tomatoes, red onion, and chopped cilantro.
3. **Make the Dressing (Optional):**
    - In a small bowl, mix Greek yogurt, lime juice, honey, salt, and pepper. Adjust seasoning to taste.
4. **Assemble the Wraps:**
    - Place a few shrimp in the center of each lettuce leaf.
    - Top with the avocado and tomato mixture.
    - Drizzle with the optional dressing if desired.

5. **Serve:**
    - Garnish with additional cilantro and lime wedges on the side.

Enjoy your fresh and vibrant Shrimp and Avocado Lettuce Wraps!

Sweet Potato and Kale Frittata

Ingredients:

- **For the Frittata:**
    - 1 large sweet potato, peeled and diced
    - 1 tablespoon olive oil
    - 1 small onion, diced
    - 2 cloves garlic, minced
    - 2 cups kale, chopped and stems removed
    - 6 large eggs
    - 1/4 cup milk (or plant-based milk)
    - 1/2 cup shredded cheddar cheese or feta cheese (optional)
    - 1/2 teaspoon dried thyme
    - Salt and pepper to taste
- **For Garnish (optional):**
    - Fresh parsley, chopped
    - Extra cheese, if desired

Instructions:

1. **Preheat Oven**: Preheat your oven to 375°F (190°C).
2. **Cook Sweet Potatoes**:
    - Heat olive oil in a large oven-safe skillet over medium heat.
    - Add diced sweet potatoes and cook, stirring occasionally, for about 8-10 minutes, until tender and lightly browned.
3. **Add Onions and Garlic**:
    - Add diced onion to the skillet and cook for another 3-4 minutes, until softened.
    - Stir in minced garlic and cook for 1 minute, until fragrant.
4. **Add Kale**:
    - Add chopped kale to the skillet and cook until wilted, about 2-3 minutes. Season with salt and pepper.
5. **Prepare Egg Mixture**:
    - In a bowl, whisk together eggs, milk, thyme, and a pinch of salt and pepper. Stir in shredded cheese if using.
6. **Combine and Cook**:
    - Pour the egg mixture over the sweet potato and kale in the skillet. Stir gently to combine.
    - Cook on the stovetop over medium heat for 2-3 minutes, or until the edges start to set.
7. **Bake**:
    - Transfer the skillet to the preheated oven and bake for 15-20 minutes, or until the frittata is fully set and the top is golden brown.

8. **Garnish and Serve**:
    - Garnish with fresh parsley and extra cheese if desired. Allow to cool slightly before slicing.

Enjoy your delicious and nutritious Sweet Potato and Kale Frittata!

Chicken and Vegetable Stir-Fry

Ingredients:

- **For the Stir-Fry:**
    - 1 lb (450 g) chicken breast or thighs, sliced into thin strips
    - 2 tablespoons vegetable oil
    - 1 red bell pepper, sliced
    - 1 yellow bell pepper, sliced
    - 1 cup broccoli florets
    - 1 cup snap peas
    - 1 carrot, thinly sliced
    - 3 green onions, chopped
    - 2 cloves garlic, minced
    - 1 tablespoon fresh ginger, minced
- **For the Sauce:**
    - 1/4 cup soy sauce or tamari
    - 2 tablespoons hoisin sauce
    - 1 tablespoon rice vinegar
    - 1 tablespoon cornstarch mixed with 2 tablespoons water (for thickening)
    - 1 tablespoon sesame oil
    - 1 teaspoon sugar or honey

Instructions:

1. **Prepare Sauce**:
    - In a small bowl, whisk together soy sauce, hoisin sauce, rice vinegar, sesame oil, sugar or honey, and the cornstarch mixture. Set aside.
2. **Cook Chicken**:
    - Heat 1 tablespoon of vegetable oil in a large skillet or wok over medium-high heat.
    - Add sliced chicken and cook until browned and cooked through, about 5-7 minutes. Remove from skillet and set aside.
3. **Stir-Fry Vegetables**:
    - In the same skillet, add the remaining vegetable oil.
    - Stir in garlic and ginger, and cook for about 1 minute until fragrant.
    - Add bell peppers, broccoli, snap peas, and carrots. Stir-fry for 4-5 minutes, or until vegetables are tender-crisp.
4. **Combine and Sauce**:
    - Return the cooked chicken to the skillet with the vegetables.
    - Pour the prepared sauce over the chicken and vegetables.
    - Stir well to coat everything in the sauce and cook for another 2-3 minutes, until the sauce thickens.

5. **Finish and Serve**:
    - Stir in chopped green onions.
    - Serve hot over rice or noodles.

Enjoy your quick and flavorful Chicken and Vegetable Stir-Fry!

Beet and Goat Cheese Salad

Ingredients:

- **For the Salad:**
    - 4 medium beets, peeled and roasted or boiled, then sliced
    - 4 cups mixed greens or arugula
    - 4 oz goat cheese, crumbled
    - 1/4 cup walnuts, toasted
    - 1/4 cup red onion, thinly sliced
    - 1/4 cup fresh parsley or basil, chopped
- **For the Dressing:**
    - 3 tablespoons olive oil
    - 1 tablespoon balsamic vinegar
    - 1 teaspoon honey or maple syrup
    - 1 teaspoon Dijon mustard
    - Salt and pepper to taste

Instructions:

1. **Prepare Beets**:
    - If using raw beets, roast them in a preheated oven at 400°F (200°C) for 45-60 minutes until tender, or boil until fork-tender. Let cool and slice.
2. **Make Dressing**:
    - Whisk together olive oil, balsamic vinegar, honey, Dijon mustard, salt, and pepper in a small bowl. Adjust seasoning as needed.
3. **Assemble Salad**:
    - In a large bowl, toss the mixed greens with a little of the dressing. Arrange the dressed greens on a serving platter or individual plates.
4. **Add Toppings**:
    - Top the greens with sliced beets, crumbled goat cheese, toasted walnuts, red onion, and chopped parsley or basil.
5. **Serve**:
    - Drizzle the remaining dressing over the salad or serve it on the side.

Enjoy your fresh and elegant Beet and Goat Cheese Salad!

Healthy Chicken Enchiladas

Ingredients:

- **For the Enchiladas:**
    - 1 lb (450 g) boneless, skinless chicken breasts
    - 1 tablespoon olive oil
    - 1 small onion, finely chopped
    - 2 cloves garlic, minced
    - 1 cup bell peppers, diced (red or green)
    - 1 cup black beans, drained and rinsed
    - 1 cup corn kernels (fresh, frozen, or canned)
    - 1 cup salsa (store-bought or homemade)
    - 1 teaspoon ground cumin
    - 1/2 teaspoon chili powder
    - Salt and pepper to taste
    - 8 small whole wheat or corn tortillas
    - 1 cup shredded reduced-fat cheddar cheese or Mexican cheese blend
- **For the Sauce (Optional):**
    - 1 cup salsa verde or enchilada sauce (store-bought or homemade)
    - 1/2 cup low-fat Greek yogurt (for a creamy texture)

Instructions:

1. **Cook the Chicken**:
    - Preheat your oven to 375°F (190°C).
    - Heat olive oil in a large skillet over medium heat.
    - Add chicken breasts and cook for 5-7 minutes per side until cooked through and no longer pink in the center. Remove from skillet and let rest for a few minutes, then shred with two forks.
2. **Prepare Filling**:
    - In the same skillet, add onion and garlic. Cook until softened, about 3-4 minutes.
    - Stir in bell peppers, black beans, and corn. Cook for another 3 minutes.
    - Add shredded chicken, salsa, cumin, chili powder, salt, and pepper. Mix well and cook for 2-3 minutes.
3. **Assemble Enchiladas**:
    - Spread a thin layer of salsa or enchilada sauce (if using) on the bottom of a baking dish.
    - Place a few tablespoons of the chicken mixture onto each tortilla, roll up tightly, and place seam-side down in the baking dish.
    - Pour remaining salsa or enchilada sauce over the top of the rolled tortillas. Sprinkle with shredded cheese.
4. **Bake**:

- Bake in the preheated oven for 20-25 minutes, or until the cheese is melted and bubbly.
5. **Serve**:
    - Garnish with chopped fresh cilantro if desired. Serve hot with a side of Greek yogurt for a healthier alternative to sour cream.

Enjoy your nutritious and flavorful Healthy Chicken Enchiladas!

Cauliflower and Chickpea Curry

Ingredients:

- **For the Curry:**
    - 1 tablespoon olive oil or coconut oil
    - 1 large onion, diced
    - 2 cloves garlic, minced
    - 1 tablespoon fresh ginger, minced
    - 1 tablespoon curry powder
    - 1 teaspoon ground cumin
    - 1/2 teaspoon ground turmeric
    - 1/2 teaspoon paprika
    - 1 can (14.5 oz) diced tomatoes
    - 1 can (15 oz) chickpeas, drained and rinsed
    - 1 small cauliflower, cut into florets
    - 1 cup coconut milk (light or full-fat)
    - Salt and pepper to taste
    - Fresh cilantro, chopped (for garnish)
- **Optional:**
    - 1 cup spinach or kale, chopped
    - 1 tablespoon lime juice

Instructions:

1. **Cook Aromatics**:
    - Heat oil in a large skillet or pot over medium heat.
    - Add onion and cook until softened, about 5 minutes.
    - Stir in garlic and ginger, cooking for another minute until fragrant.
2. **Add Spices**:
    - Add curry powder, cumin, turmeric, and paprika. Cook for 1-2 minutes, stirring frequently, until the spices are fragrant.
3. **Add Tomatoes and Cauliflower**:
    - Stir in the diced tomatoes and cauliflower florets. Cook for 5 minutes, allowing the flavors to meld.
4. **Simmer**:
    - Add chickpeas and coconut milk. Bring to a simmer and cook for 15-20 minutes, or until the cauliflower is tender and the sauce has thickened.
5. **Finish**:
    - If using, stir in spinach or kale and cook for an additional 2-3 minutes until wilted.
    - Adjust seasoning with salt, pepper, and lime juice if desired.
6. **Serve**:
    - Garnish with fresh cilantro. Serve hot over rice or with naan.

Enjoy your hearty and flavorful Cauliflower and Chickpea Curry!

Grilled Shrimp and Pineapple Skewers

Ingredients:

- **For the Marinade:**
    - 1/4 cup olive oil
    - 3 tablespoons lime juice (about 1 lime)
    - 2 tablespoons honey or maple syrup
    - 2 cloves garlic, minced
    - 1 teaspoon ground cumin
    - 1/2 teaspoon paprika
    - 1/2 teaspoon ground coriander
    - Salt and pepper to taste
- **For the Skewers:**
    - 1 lb (450 g) large shrimp, peeled and deveined
    - 2 cups fresh pineapple, cut into 1-inch chunks
    - 1 red bell pepper, cut into 1-inch pieces
    - 1 green bell pepper, cut into 1-inch pieces
    - 1 small red onion, cut into 1-inch pieces
    - Fresh cilantro, chopped (for garnish)
    - Lime wedges (for serving)

Instructions:

1. **Prepare Marinade**:
    - In a bowl, whisk together olive oil, lime juice, honey, garlic, cumin, paprika, coriander, salt, and pepper.
2. **Marinate Shrimp**:
    - Place the shrimp in a resealable plastic bag or shallow dish. Pour half of the marinade over the shrimp, reserving the other half for basting. Marinate in the refrigerator for 15-30 minutes.
3. **Prepare Skewers**:
    - If using wooden skewers, soak them in water for at least 30 minutes to prevent burning.
    - Thread shrimp, pineapple chunks, bell peppers, and red onion onto skewers, alternating between each ingredient.
4. **Preheat Grill**:
    - Preheat your grill to medium-high heat.
5. **Grill Skewers**:
    - Place the skewers on the grill and cook for 2-3 minutes per side, or until the shrimp are pink and opaque, and the pineapple is caramelized. Brush with the reserved marinade during grilling.
6. **Serve**:

- - Remove from the grill and garnish with chopped cilantro.
  - Serve with lime wedges on the side.

Enjoy your flavorful and tropical Grilled Shrimp and Pineapple Skewers!

Stuffed Acorn Squash with Wild Rice

Ingredients:

- **For the Stuffed Squash:**
    - 2 medium acorn squashes
    - 1 tablespoon olive oil
    - 1 small onion, diced
    - 2 cloves garlic, minced
    - 1 cup wild rice, cooked according to package instructions
    - 1/2 cup dried cranberries or raisins
    - 1/2 cup walnuts or pecans, chopped
    - 1/2 cup fresh parsley or sage, chopped
    - 1/2 teaspoon ground cinnamon
    - Salt and pepper to taste
    - 1/2 cup crumbled feta cheese or shredded Parmesan cheese (optional)
- **For Garnish (optional):**
    - Fresh parsley or sage leaves
    - Additional nuts or cheese

Instructions:

1. **Preheat Oven**:
    - Preheat your oven to 400°F (200°C).
2. **Prepare Squash**:
    - Cut each acorn squash in half and scoop out the seeds. Place the squash halves cut-side up on a baking sheet. Brush with olive oil and season with salt and pepper.
    - Roast in the preheated oven for 25-30 minutes, or until the squash is tender when pierced with a fork.
3. **Prepare Filling**:
    - While the squash is roasting, heat olive oil in a skillet over medium heat. Add diced onion and cook until softened, about 5 minutes.
    - Stir in minced garlic and cook for 1 minute until fragrant.
    - In a large bowl, combine the cooked wild rice, dried cranberries or raisins, chopped nuts, chopped parsley or sage, cinnamon, and the cooked onion and garlic. Season with salt and pepper to taste.
4. **Stuff Squash**:
    - Remove the roasted squash from the oven. Spoon the wild rice mixture into each squash half, packing it in gently.
    - If using, sprinkle the tops with crumbled feta cheese or shredded Parmesan.
5. **Bake Again**:

- Return the stuffed squash to the oven and bake for an additional 10-15 minutes, or until the cheese is melted and bubbly, and the stuffing is heated through.
6. **Serve**:
    - Garnish with additional fresh parsley or sage and nuts or cheese if desired.

Enjoy your hearty and nutritious Stuffed Acorn Squash with Wild Rice!

Spicy Chickpea and Spinach Stew

Ingredients:

- **For the Stew:**
    - 1 tablespoon olive oil
    - 1 large onion, diced
    - 3 cloves garlic, minced
    - 1 tablespoon fresh ginger, minced
    - 1-2 tablespoons curry powder (adjust to taste)
    - 1 teaspoon ground cumin
    - 1/2 teaspoon paprika
    - 1/4 teaspoon cayenne pepper (optional, for extra heat)
    - 1 can (14.5 oz) diced tomatoes
    - 1 can (15 oz) chickpeas, drained and rinsed
    - 1 cup vegetable broth
    - 4 cups fresh spinach, chopped
    - Salt and pepper to taste
    - 1 tablespoon lemon juice (optional, for brightness)
- **For Garnish (optional):**
    - Fresh cilantro, chopped
    - Plain yogurt or dairy-free alternative

Instructions:

1. **Cook Aromatics**:
    - Heat olive oil in a large pot over medium heat.
    - Add diced onion and cook until softened, about 5 minutes.
    - Stir in garlic and ginger, and cook for an additional minute until fragrant.
2. **Add Spices**:
    - Add curry powder, cumin, paprika, and cayenne pepper (if using). Cook for 1-2 minutes, stirring frequently, to toast the spices.
3. **Add Tomatoes and Chickpeas**:
    - Stir in the diced tomatoes and chickpeas. Cook for 2-3 minutes.
4. **Simmer**:
    - Pour in the vegetable broth and bring the mixture to a simmer. Cook for 10-15 minutes, allowing the flavors to meld and the stew to thicken slightly.
5. **Add Spinach**:
    - Stir in the chopped spinach and cook until wilted, about 2-3 minutes. Season with salt and pepper to taste.
6. **Finish**:
    - Stir in lemon juice if desired for added brightness.
7. **Serve**:

- Garnish with fresh cilantro and a dollop of yogurt if using. Serve hot.

Enjoy your flavorful and comforting Spicy Chickpea and Spinach Stew!

Garlic Herb Grilled Chicken

Ingredients:

- **For the Marinade:**
    - 1/4 cup olive oil
    - 3 cloves garlic, minced
    - 2 tablespoons fresh rosemary or thyme, chopped (or a mix of both)
    - 1 tablespoon fresh lemon juice
    - 1 teaspoon Dijon mustard
    - 1 teaspoon honey
    - Salt and pepper to taste
- **For the Chicken:**
    - 4 boneless, skinless chicken breasts

Instructions:

1. **Prepare Marinade**:
    - In a bowl, whisk together olive oil, minced garlic, chopped rosemary or thyme, lemon juice, Dijon mustard, honey, salt, and pepper.
2. **Marinate Chicken**:
    - Place the chicken breasts in a resealable plastic bag or shallow dish. Pour the marinade over the chicken, ensuring it's well-coated.
    - Seal the bag or cover the dish and refrigerate for at least 30 minutes, up to 4 hours for more flavor.
3. **Preheat Grill**:
    - Preheat your grill to medium-high heat.
4. **Grill Chicken**:
    - Remove the chicken from the marinade and discard any excess marinade.
    - Grill the chicken for 6-8 minutes per side, or until fully cooked and the internal temperature reaches 165°F (74°C).
5. **Rest and Serve**:
    - Let the chicken rest for a few minutes before slicing.

Enjoy your juicy and flavorful Garlic Herb Grilled Chicken!

Mango and Black Bean Salad

Ingredients:

- **For the Marinade:**
    - 1/4 cup olive oil
    - 3 cloves garlic, minced
    - 2 tablespoons fresh rosemary or thyme, chopped (or a mix of both)
    - 1 tablespoon fresh lemon juice
    - 1 teaspoon Dijon mustard
    - 1 teaspoon honey
    - Salt and pepper to taste
- **For the Chicken:**
    - 4 boneless, skinless chicken breasts

Instructions:

1. **Prepare Marinade**:
    - In a bowl, whisk together olive oil, minced garlic, chopped rosemary or thyme, lemon juice, Dijon mustard, honey, salt, and pepper.
2. **Marinate Chicken**:
    - Place the chicken breasts in a resealable plastic bag or shallow dish. Pour the marinade over the chicken, ensuring it's well-coated.
    - Seal the bag or cover the dish and refrigerate for at least 30 minutes, up to 4 hours for more flavor.
3. **Preheat Grill**:
    - Preheat your grill to medium-high heat.
4. **Grill Chicken**:
    - Remove the chicken from the marinade and discard any excess marinade.
    - Grill the chicken for 6-8 minutes per side, or until fully cooked and the internal temperature reaches 165°F (74°C).
5. **Rest and Serve**:
    - Let the chicken rest for a few minutes before slicing.

Enjoy your juicy and flavorful Garlic Herb Grilled Chicken!

Mango and Black Bean Salad
Ingredients:
For the Salad:

1 ripe mango, peeled, pitted, and diced
1 can (15 oz) black beans, drained and rinsed
1 red bell pepper, diced
1/2 red onion, finely chopped
1/4 cup fresh cilantro, chopped
1 avocado, diced
1 cup corn kernels (fresh, frozen, or canned)
1 lime, juiced
For the Dressing:

2 tablespoons olive oil
1 tablespoon lime juice (additional)
1 teaspoon honey or maple syrup
1/2 teaspoon ground cumin
Salt and pepper to taste
Instructions:
Prepare Salad Ingredients:

In a large bowl, combine diced mango, black beans, red bell pepper, red onion, cilantro, avocado, and corn.
Make Dressing:

In a small bowl or jar, whisk together olive oil, lime juice, honey, cumin, salt, and pepper.
Combine:

Pour the dressing over the salad and gently toss to combine.
Serve:

Serve immediately, or chill in the refrigerator for 30 minutes to allow flavors to meld.
Enjoy your refreshing and vibrant Mango and Black Bean Salad!

Roasted Red Pepper and Tomato Soup

Ingredients:

- **For the Soup:**
    - 4 large red bell peppers
    - 6 ripe tomatoes, halved
    - 1 tablespoon olive oil
    - 1 large onion, chopped
    - 3 cloves garlic, minced
    - 2 cups vegetable broth
    - 1 teaspoon dried basil or 1 tablespoon fresh basil, chopped
    - 1/2 teaspoon dried oregano
    - Salt and pepper to taste
    - 1/4 cup heavy cream or coconut milk (optional, for creaminess)

Instructions:

1. **Roast Peppers and Tomatoes**:
    - Preheat your oven to 425°F (220°C).
    - Place the red bell peppers and tomato halves on a baking sheet. Drizzle with olive oil and season with salt and pepper.
    - Roast for 25-30 minutes, or until the peppers and tomatoes are tender and slightly charred. Remove from oven and let cool.
2. **Prepare Soup Base**:
    - Peel and discard the skin from the roasted peppers.
    - In a large pot, heat a tablespoon of olive oil over medium heat.
    - Add the chopped onion and cook until softened, about 5 minutes.
    - Stir in the minced garlic and cook for another minute.
3. **Combine Ingredients**:
    - Add the roasted peppers and tomatoes to the pot. Stir in the vegetable broth, basil, and oregano. Bring to a simmer and cook for 10 minutes to meld flavors.
4. **Blend Soup**:
    - Use an immersion blender to puree the soup until smooth, or carefully transfer to a blender in batches. Return to the pot if using a blender.
5. **Finish**:
    - Stir in heavy cream or coconut milk if desired. Adjust seasoning with salt and pepper.
6. **Serve**:
    - Serve hot, garnished with fresh basil if desired.

Enjoy your rich and comforting Roasted Red Pepper and Tomato Soup!

Quinoa and Black Bean Burrito Bowls

Ingredients:

- **For the Bowls:**
    - 1 cup quinoa
    - 2 cups water or vegetable broth
    - 1 can (15 oz) black beans, drained and rinsed
    - 1 cup corn kernels (fresh, frozen, or canned)
    - 1 cup cherry tomatoes, halved
    - 1 avocado, diced
    - 1/2 cup red onion, finely chopped
    - 1/2 cup fresh cilantro, chopped
    - 1 lime, cut into wedges
- **For the Dressing:**
    - 3 tablespoons olive oil
    - 2 tablespoons lime juice
    - 1 teaspoon honey or maple syrup
    - 1 teaspoon ground cumin
    - 1/2 teaspoon smoked paprika
    - Salt and pepper to taste

Instructions:

1. **Cook Quinoa**:
    - Rinse quinoa under cold water.
    - In a medium saucepan, bring water or vegetable broth to a boil. Add quinoa, reduce heat to low, cover, and simmer for 15 minutes, or until quinoa is tender and the liquid is absorbed. Fluff with a fork and let cool slightly.
2. **Prepare Dressing**:
    - In a small bowl, whisk together olive oil, lime juice, honey, cumin, smoked paprika, salt, and pepper.
3. **Assemble Bowls**:
    - In serving bowls, layer cooked quinoa, black beans, corn, cherry tomatoes, avocado, red onion, and cilantro.
4. **Add Dressing**:
    - Drizzle the dressing over the bowls and toss gently to combine.
5. **Serve**:
    - Garnish with lime wedges for added flavor.

Enjoy your vibrant and nutritious Quinoa and Black Bean Burrito Bowls!

Thai Beef Salad

Ingredients:

- **For the Salad:**
    - 1 lb (450 g) beef sirloin or flank steak
    - 1 tablespoon olive oil or vegetable oil
    - 4 cups mixed salad greens or shredded lettuce
    - 1 cup cherry tomatoes, halved
    - 1 cucumber, thinly sliced
    - 1/2 red onion, thinly sliced
    - 1/2 cup fresh cilantro, chopped
    - 1/4 cup fresh mint leaves, chopped
    - 1/4 cup roasted peanuts or cashews (optional, for garnish)
- **For the Dressing:**
    - 3 tablespoons lime juice (about 2 limes)
    - 2 tablespoons fish sauce
    - 1 tablespoon soy sauce or tamari
    - 1 tablespoon brown sugar or honey
    - 1-2 cloves garlic, minced
    - 1 small red chili or 1/2 teaspoon red chili flakes (adjust to taste)

Instructions:

1. **Prepare Beef**:
    - Preheat a grill or grill pan over medium-high heat.
    - Rub the beef with a bit of oil, salt, and pepper.
    - Grill the beef for 4-6 minutes per side, or until desired doneness is reached (medium-rare is recommended).
    - Let the beef rest for a few minutes before slicing thinly against the grain.
2. **Make Dressing**:
    - In a small bowl, whisk together lime juice, fish sauce, soy sauce, brown sugar, minced garlic, and red chili or chili flakes. Adjust seasoning to taste.
3. **Assemble Salad**:
    - In a large bowl, combine salad greens, cherry tomatoes, cucumber, red onion, cilantro, and mint.
    - Toss with a little of the dressing to lightly coat the vegetables.
4. **Add Beef**:
    - Arrange the sliced beef on top of the salad.
    - Drizzle with additional dressing as desired.
5. **Garnish and Serve**:
    - Garnish with roasted peanuts or cashews if using.
    - Serve immediately.

Enjoy your refreshing and flavorful Thai Beef Salad!

Lemon Dill Salmon with Roasted Veggies

Ingredients:

- **For the Salmon:**
    - 4 salmon fillets
    - 2 tablespoons olive oil
    - 1 lemon, thinly sliced
    - 2 tablespoons fresh dill, chopped (or 2 teaspoons dried dill)
    - 2 cloves garlic, minced
    - Salt and pepper to taste
- **For the Roasted Veggies:**
    - 2 cups baby potatoes, halved
    - 1 cup carrots, sliced
    - 1 cup bell peppers, diced
    - 1 tablespoon olive oil
    - 1 teaspoon dried thyme
    - 1 teaspoon dried rosemary
    - Salt and pepper to taste

Instructions:

1. **Preheat Oven**:
    - Preheat your oven to 400°F (200°C).
2. **Prepare Roasted Veggies**:
    - Toss the baby potatoes, carrots, and bell peppers with olive oil, thyme, rosemary, salt, and pepper.
    - Spread the veggies on a baking sheet and roast for 20-25 minutes, or until tender and starting to brown.
3. **Prepare Salmon**:
    - While the veggies are roasting, place the salmon fillets on a separate baking sheet lined with parchment paper.
    - Drizzle with olive oil and sprinkle with minced garlic, dill, salt, and pepper.
    - Top each fillet with lemon slices.
4. **Bake Salmon**:
    - Place the salmon in the oven during the last 10-12 minutes of the veggies' roasting time. Bake until the salmon is cooked through and flakes easily with a fork.
5. **Serve**:
    - Serve the lemon dill salmon alongside the roasted veggies.

Enjoy your healthy and flavorful Lemon Dill Salmon with Roasted Veggies!

Chicken and Avocado Salad

Ingredients:

- **For the Salad:**
    - 2 cups cooked chicken breast, diced or shredded (grilled, baked, or poached)
    - 1 large avocado, diced
    - 1 cup cherry tomatoes, halved
    - 1/2 cucumber, diced
    - 1/4 red onion, finely chopped
    - 1/4 cup fresh cilantro or parsley, chopped
    - 4 cups mixed greens or lettuce
- **For the Dressing:**
    - 3 tablespoons olive oil
    - 2 tablespoons lime juice (about 1 lime)
    - 1 tablespoon Dijon mustard
    - 1 teaspoon honey or maple syrup
    - Salt and pepper to taste

Instructions:

1. **Prepare Salad Ingredients**:
    - In a large bowl, combine diced chicken, avocado, cherry tomatoes, cucumber, red onion, and fresh cilantro or parsley.
2. **Make Dressing**:
    - In a small bowl or jar, whisk together olive oil, lime juice, Dijon mustard, honey, salt, and pepper.
3. **Assemble Salad**:
    - Arrange mixed greens or lettuce on a serving platter or individual plates.
    - Top with the chicken and avocado mixture.
    - Drizzle with the dressing and gently toss to combine.
4. **Serve**:
    - Serve immediately, or chill in the refrigerator for up to an hour before serving.

Enjoy your fresh and nutritious Chicken and Avocado Salad!

Lentil and Spinach Soup

Ingredients:

- **For the Soup:**
    - 1 tablespoon olive oil
    - 1 large onion, chopped
    - 2 cloves garlic, minced
    - 2 carrots, diced
    - 2 celery stalks, diced
    - 1 cup dried green or brown lentils, rinsed
    - 1 can (14.5 oz) diced tomatoes
    - 6 cups vegetable broth
    - 1 teaspoon ground cumin
    - 1/2 teaspoon paprika
    - 1/2 teaspoon dried thyme
    - Salt and pepper to taste
    - 4 cups fresh spinach, chopped
    - 1 tablespoon lemon juice (optional, for brightness)

Instructions:

1. **Cook Aromatics**:
    - Heat olive oil in a large pot over medium heat.
    - Add chopped onion, carrots, and celery. Cook until softened, about 5-7 minutes.
    - Stir in minced garlic and cook for another minute.
2. **Add Lentils and Spices**:
    - Add the rinsed lentils, diced tomatoes, vegetable broth, cumin, paprika, thyme, salt, and pepper.
3. **Simmer**:
    - Bring to a boil, then reduce heat to low and simmer for 25-30 minutes, or until lentils are tender.
4. **Add Spinach**:
    - Stir in chopped spinach and cook for 2-3 minutes, until wilted.
5. **Finish**:
    - Add lemon juice if desired. Adjust seasoning with salt and pepper.
6. **Serve**:
    - Serve hot, with crusty bread if desired.

Enjoy your hearty and nutritious Lentil and Spinach Soup!

Grilled Veggie and Hummus Wrap

Ingredients:

- **For the Wrap:**
    - 1 zucchini, sliced into thin strips
    - 1 red bell pepper, sliced into thin strips
    - 1 yellow bell pepper, sliced into thin strips
    - 1 small eggplant, sliced into thin strips
    - 1 tablespoon olive oil
    - Salt and pepper to taste
    - 4 large whole wheat or flour tortillas
    - 1 cup hummus (store-bought or homemade)
    - 1 cup baby spinach or mixed greens
    - 1/4 cup crumbled feta cheese or shredded cheese (optional)
- **For Optional Toppings:**
    - Sliced avocado
    - Sliced olives
    - Sliced cucumbers

Instructions:

1. **Grill Veggies**:
    - Preheat your grill or grill pan to medium-high heat.
    - Toss the zucchini, bell peppers, and eggplant with olive oil, salt, and pepper.
    - Grill the vegetables for 3-4 minutes per side, or until tender and slightly charred. Remove from the grill and set aside.
2. **Prepare Wraps**:
    - Spread a generous layer of hummus on each tortilla.
    - Layer the grilled veggies on top of the hummus.
    - Add a handful of spinach or mixed greens, and sprinkle with crumbled feta cheese if using.
3. **Add Optional Toppings**:
    - Add any additional toppings like avocado, olives, or cucumbers if desired.
4. **Roll and Serve**:
    - Roll up the tortillas tightly, folding in the sides as you go.
    - Slice in half and serve immediately, or wrap in foil for a portable lunch.

Enjoy your flavorful and satisfying Grilled Veggie and Hummus Wrap!

Mediterranean Quinoa Salad

Ingredients:

- **For the Salad:**
    - 1 cup quinoa
    - 2 cups water or vegetable broth
    - 1 cup cherry tomatoes, halved
    - 1 cucumber, diced
    - 1/2 red onion, finely chopped
    - 1/2 cup Kalamata olives, pitted and sliced
    - 1/2 cup feta cheese, crumbled
    - 1/4 cup fresh parsley, chopped
    - 1/4 cup fresh mint, chopped (optional)
- **For the Dressing:**
    - 1/4 cup olive oil
    - 2 tablespoons red wine vinegar
    - 1 tablespoon lemon juice
    - 1 teaspoon Dijon mustard
    - 1 clove garlic, minced
    - 1/2 teaspoon dried oregano
    - Salt and pepper to taste

Instructions:

1. **Cook Quinoa**:
    - Rinse the quinoa under cold water.
    - In a medium saucepan, bring water or vegetable broth to a boil.
    - Add quinoa, reduce heat to low, cover, and simmer for 15 minutes, or until quinoa is tender and liquid is absorbed. Fluff with a fork and let cool.
2. **Prepare Dressing**:
    - In a small bowl or jar, whisk together olive oil, red wine vinegar, lemon juice, Dijon mustard, minced garlic, dried oregano, salt, and pepper.
3. **Assemble Salad**:
    - In a large bowl, combine cooked quinoa, cherry tomatoes, cucumber, red onion, olives, feta cheese, parsley, and mint.
4. **Add Dressing**:
    - Drizzle the dressing over the salad and toss to combine.
5. **Serve**:
    - Serve immediately or chill in the refrigerator for up to 2 hours to allow flavors to meld.

Enjoy your fresh and vibrant Mediterranean Quinoa Salad!

Teriyaki Salmon with Broccoli

Ingredients:

- **For the Salmon:**
    - 4 salmon fillets
    - 1/4 cup teriyaki sauce
    - 2 tablespoons soy sauce or tamari
    - 1 tablespoon honey or maple syrup
    - 1 tablespoon sesame oil
    - 1 teaspoon grated ginger
    - 1 clove garlic, minced
    - Sesame seeds and chopped green onions for garnish (optional)
- **For the Broccoli:**
    - 2 cups broccoli florets
    - 1 tablespoon olive oil
    - Salt and pepper to taste

Instructions:

1. **Marinate Salmon**:
    - In a bowl, mix teriyaki sauce, soy sauce, honey, sesame oil, ginger, and garlic.
    - Place the salmon fillets in a shallow dish and pour the marinade over them.
    - Cover and refrigerate for at least 15-30 minutes.
2. **Preheat Oven**:
    - Preheat your oven to 400°F (200°C).
3. **Prepare Broccoli**:
    - Toss broccoli florets with olive oil, salt, and pepper.
    - Spread on a baking sheet and roast in the oven for 15-20 minutes, or until tender and slightly crispy.
4. **Cook Salmon**:
    - Place the marinated salmon fillets on a separate baking sheet lined with parchment paper.
    - Bake in the oven for 12-15 minutes, or until the salmon is cooked through and flakes easily with a fork.
5. **Serve**:
    - Serve the salmon topped with sesame seeds and chopped green onions if desired, alongside the roasted broccoli.

Enjoy your flavorful and healthy Teriyaki Salmon with Broccoli!

Butternut Squash and Black Bean Chili

Ingredients:

- **For the Chili:**
    - 1 tablespoon olive oil
    - 1 large onion, diced
    - 3 cloves garlic, minced
    - 1 bell pepper, diced (any color)
    - 1 medium butternut squash, peeled, seeded, and cubed
    - 2 cans (15 oz each) black beans, drained and rinsed
    - 1 can (14.5 oz) diced tomatoes
    - 2 cups vegetable broth
    - 1 tablespoon chili powder
    - 1 teaspoon ground cumin
    - 1/2 teaspoon smoked paprika
    - 1/4 teaspoon cayenne pepper (optional, for extra heat)
    - Salt and pepper to taste
- **For Garnish (optional):**
    - Fresh cilantro, chopped
    - Sliced avocado
    - Shredded cheese
    - Sour cream or Greek yogurt
    - Lime wedges

Instructions:

1. **Cook Aromatics**:
    - Heat olive oil in a large pot over medium heat.
    - Add diced onion and cook until softened, about 5 minutes.
    - Stir in minced garlic and bell pepper, cooking for an additional 2-3 minutes.
2. **Add Butternut Squash**:
    - Add cubed butternut squash to the pot. Cook for about 5 minutes, stirring occasionally.
3. **Add Beans and Tomatoes**:
    - Stir in black beans, diced tomatoes, and vegetable broth.
4. **Season and Simmer**:
    - Add chili powder, ground cumin, smoked paprika, cayenne pepper (if using), salt, and pepper.
    - Bring the mixture to a boil, then reduce heat and simmer for 25-30 minutes, or until the butternut squash is tender and the chili has thickened.
5. **Finish and Serve**:
    - Taste and adjust seasoning if needed.

- Serve hot, garnished with fresh cilantro, sliced avocado, shredded cheese, sour cream, and lime wedges if desired.

Enjoy your hearty and nutritious Butternut Squash and Black Bean Chili!

Grilled Tofu with Peanut Sauce

Ingredients:

- **For the Grilled Tofu:**
    - 1 block (14 oz) extra-firm tofu
    - 2 tablespoons soy sauce or tamari
    - 1 tablespoon olive oil
    - 1 tablespoon maple syrup or honey
    - 1 teaspoon garlic powder
    - 1 teaspoon ground ginger
- **For the Peanut Sauce:**
    - 1/4 cup creamy peanut butter
    - 2 tablespoons soy sauce or tamari
    - 2 tablespoons rice vinegar
    - 1 tablespoon honey or maple syrup
    - 1 clove garlic, minced
    - 1 teaspoon grated ginger
    - 2-3 tablespoons water (to thin the sauce)
    - Red pepper flakes (optional, for heat)

Instructions:

1. **Prepare Tofu:**
    - Drain and press the tofu to remove excess moisture. Cut it into 1/2-inch thick slices or cubes.
    - In a small bowl, mix soy sauce, olive oil, maple syrup, garlic powder, and ground ginger.
    - Marinate the tofu in this mixture for at least 15 minutes, turning occasionally.
2. **Prepare Peanut Sauce:**
    - In a bowl, whisk together peanut butter, soy sauce, rice vinegar, honey, minced garlic, and grated ginger.
    - Add water a little at a time until the sauce reaches your desired consistency. Adjust seasoning with red pepper flakes if desired.
3. **Grill Tofu:**
    - Preheat your grill or grill pan to medium-high heat.
    - Place the marinated tofu on the grill. Grill for 4-5 minutes per side, or until grill marks appear and the tofu is heated through.
4. **Serve:**
    - Drizzle the grilled tofu with peanut sauce or serve the sauce on the side for dipping.

Enjoy your delicious and savory Grilled Tofu with Peanut Sauce!

Spinach and Feta Stuffed Chicken

Ingredients:

- **For the Chicken:**
    - 4 boneless, skinless chicken breasts
    - 1 tablespoon olive oil
    - 1 cup fresh spinach, chopped
    - 1/2 cup feta cheese, crumbled
    - 2 cloves garlic, minced
    - 1/4 teaspoon dried oregano
    - Salt and pepper to taste
    - Toothpicks or kitchen twine
- **For the Optional Seasoning:**
    - 1 teaspoon paprika
    - 1 teaspoon dried thyme

Instructions:

1. **Prepare Filling:**
    - In a medium skillet, heat olive oil over medium heat.
    - Add minced garlic and cook for 1 minute until fragrant.
    - Stir in chopped spinach and cook until wilted, about 2-3 minutes.
    - Remove from heat and mix in crumbled feta cheese. Season with oregano, salt, and pepper.
2. **Prepare Chicken:**
    - Preheat your oven to 375°F (190°C).
    - Using a sharp knife, make a pocket in each chicken breast by cutting horizontally, but not all the way through.
    - Stuff each pocket with the spinach and feta mixture. Secure with toothpicks or kitchen twine to keep the filling inside.
3. **Season and Bake:**
    - Season the outside of the chicken breasts with salt, pepper, paprika, and thyme if using.
    - Heat a bit of olive oil in an oven-safe skillet over medium-high heat.
    - Sear the chicken breasts for 2-3 minutes per side until golden brown.
    - Transfer the skillet to the oven and bake for 20-25 minutes, or until the chicken is cooked through and reaches an internal temperature of 165°F (74°C).
4. **Serve:**
    - Remove toothpicks or twine before serving.

Enjoy your flavorful and juicy Spinach and Feta Stuffed Chicken!

Sweet Potato Black Bean Burgers:

Ingredients:

- **For the Burgers:**
    - 1 large sweet potato, peeled and cubed
    - 1 can (15 oz) black beans, drained and rinsed
    - 1/2 cup cooked quinoa (optional, for added texture)
    - 1/4 cup finely chopped red onion
    - 1 clove garlic, minced
    - 1/2 teaspoon ground cumin
    - 1/2 teaspoon paprika
    - 1/4 teaspoon chili powder
    - 1 egg (or flax egg for a vegan option)
    - 1/2 cup breadcrumbs (or gluten-free breadcrumbs)
    - Salt and pepper to taste
    - Olive oil for cooking
- **For Serving:**
    - Burger buns
    - Lettuce
    - Tomato slices
    - Avocado slices
    - Your favorite burger toppings and condiments

Instructions:

1. **Cook Sweet Potato:**
    - Preheat oven to 400°F (200°C).
    - Toss sweet potato cubes with a bit of olive oil, salt, and pepper. Spread on a baking sheet and roast for 25-30 minutes, until tender. Let cool slightly.
2. **Mash and Mix:**
    - In a large bowl, mash the roasted sweet potato with a fork or potato masher.
    - Add black beans and mash them together with the sweet potato, leaving some beans whole for texture.
    - Stir in cooked quinoa, red onion, garlic, cumin, paprika, chili powder, and salt and pepper.
3. **Form Patties:**
    - Add the egg and breadcrumbs to the mixture and stir until well combined. If the mixture is too wet, add more breadcrumbs until it holds together.
    - Form the mixture into 4-6 patties, depending on your preferred size.
4. **Cook Burgers:**
    - Heat a bit of olive oil in a skillet over medium heat.

- Cook the patties for 4-5 minutes per side, or until golden brown and crispy on the outside.

5. **Assemble and Serve:**
    - Serve the burgers on buns with your choice of lettuce, tomato, avocado, and other toppings.

Enjoy your hearty and delicious Sweet Potato Black Bean Burgers!

Roasted Turkey and Veggie Wrap

Ingredients:

- **For the Wrap:**
    - 4 large whole wheat or flour tortillas
    - 8 oz (225 g) roasted turkey breast, sliced
    - 1 cup roasted red peppers, sliced
    - 1 cup fresh spinach or mixed greens
    - 1 cup sliced cucumber
    - 1/2 cup shredded carrots
    - 1/4 cup red onion, thinly sliced
    - 1 avocado, sliced
    - 1/4 cup crumbled feta cheese (optional)
- **For the Dressing (optional):**
    - 1/4 cup Greek yogurt
    - 1 tablespoon Dijon mustard
    - 1 tablespoon lemon juice
    - 1 teaspoon honey
    - Salt and pepper to taste

Instructions:

1. **Prepare Dressing (if using):**
    - In a small bowl, whisk together Greek yogurt, Dijon mustard, lemon juice, honey, salt, and pepper until smooth. Set aside.
2. **Assemble Wraps:**
    - Lay the tortillas flat on a clean surface.
    - Spread a thin layer of the dressing (if using) on each tortilla.
    - Layer the roasted turkey slices evenly on each tortilla.
    - Top with roasted red peppers, spinach or mixed greens, cucumber slices, shredded carrots, red onion, and avocado slices.
    - Sprinkle with crumbled feta cheese if desired.
3. **Roll and Slice:**
    - Carefully roll up each tortilla tightly, tucking in the sides as you go to keep the filling inside.
    - Slice the wraps in half diagonally.
4. **Serve:**
    - Serve immediately, or wrap in foil or plastic wrap for an on-the-go meal.

Enjoy your flavorful and satisfying Roasted Turkey and Veggie Wrap!

Spaghetti Squash Carbonara

Ingredients:

- **For the Carbonara:**
    - 1 medium spaghetti squash
    - 4 slices bacon or pancetta, diced
    - 2 cloves garlic, minced
    - 2 large eggs
    - 1/2 cup grated Parmesan cheese
    - 1/4 cup chopped fresh parsley
    - Salt and pepper to taste
- **Optional for Extra Flavor:**
    - 1/4 teaspoon red pepper flakes
    - 1/4 cup frozen peas (thawed)

Instructions:

1. **Prepare Spaghetti Squash:**
    - Preheat your oven to 400°F (200°C).
    - Cut the spaghetti squash in half lengthwise and scoop out the seeds.
    - Place the squash halves cut-side down on a baking sheet and roast for 40-45 minutes, or until tender. Let cool slightly.
    - Use a fork to scrape out the spaghetti-like strands and set aside.
2. **Cook Bacon:**
    - In a large skillet, cook diced bacon or pancetta over medium heat until crispy. Remove with a slotted spoon and set aside, leaving the rendered fat in the skillet.
3. **Cook Garlic:**
    - Add minced garlic to the skillet and cook for about 1 minute, until fragrant.
4. **Combine Carbonara Ingredients:**
    - In a bowl, whisk together eggs, Parmesan cheese, and black pepper.
    - Add the cooked spaghetti squash to the skillet with the garlic. Toss to coat with the bacon fat.
5. **Mix with Egg Mixture:**
    - Remove the skillet from heat and quickly toss the spaghetti squash with the egg mixture, allowing the residual heat to create a creamy sauce.
    - Stir in cooked bacon and chopped parsley. Add peas if using.
6. **Serve:**
    - Serve immediately, garnished with additional Parmesan cheese and fresh parsley if desired.

Enjoy your delicious and healthier Spaghetti Squash Carbonara!

Asian-Inspired Chicken Salad

Ingredients:

- **For the Salad:**
    - 2 cups cooked chicken breast, shredded or diced
    - 4 cups mixed greens or shredded cabbage
    - 1 cup snap peas or sugar snap peas, trimmed
    - 1/2 cup shredded carrots
    - 1/2 cup red bell pepper, thinly sliced
    - 1/4 cup sliced almonds (toasted if desired)
    - 1/4 cup chopped fresh cilantro
    - 1/4 cup thinly sliced green onions
- **For the Dressing:**
    - 1/4 cup soy sauce or tamari
    - 2 tablespoons rice vinegar
    - 2 tablespoons sesame oil
    - 1 tablespoon honey or maple syrup
    - 1 teaspoon grated ginger
    - 1 clove garlic, minced
    - 1 teaspoon sesame seeds (optional)

Instructions:

1. **Prepare Salad Ingredients:**
    - In a large bowl, combine shredded or diced chicken, mixed greens or shredded cabbage, snap peas, shredded carrots, red bell pepper, almonds, cilantro, and green onions.
2. **Make Dressing:**
    - In a small bowl or jar, whisk together soy sauce, rice vinegar, sesame oil, honey, grated ginger, garlic, and sesame seeds if using.
3. **Toss Salad:**
    - Drizzle the dressing over the salad and toss to combine.
4. **Serve:**
    - Serve immediately, or chill in the refrigerator for up to an hour before serving.

Enjoy your fresh and flavorful Asian-Inspired Chicken Salad!

Creamy Avocado and Cucumber Soup

Ingredients:

- **For the Soup:**
    - 2 ripe avocados, peeled and pitted
    - 1 large cucumber, peeled and chopped
    - 1 cup plain Greek yogurt or coconut yogurt
    - 1 cup vegetable broth (chilled or at room temperature)
    - 2 tablespoons fresh lime juice
    - 2 cloves garlic, minced
    - 1/4 cup fresh cilantro or parsley, chopped
    - Salt and pepper to taste
- **For Garnish (optional):**
    - Sliced radishes
    - Chopped chives
    - Extra cilantro or parsley
    - A drizzle of olive oil

Instructions:

1. **Blend Ingredients:**
    - In a blender or food processor, combine avocados, cucumber, Greek yogurt, vegetable broth, lime juice, garlic, and fresh cilantro or parsley. Blend until smooth and creamy.
2. **Season:**
    - Taste and season with salt and pepper. Blend again to combine.
3. **Chill:**
    - Transfer the soup to a bowl or container and chill in the refrigerator for at least 30 minutes, or until cold.
4. **Serve:**
    - Serve chilled, garnished with sliced radishes, chopped chives, extra cilantro or parsley, and a drizzle of olive oil if desired.

Enjoy your refreshing and creamy Avocado and Cucumber Soup!

www.ingramcontent.com/pod-product-compliance
Lightning Source LLC
LaVergne TN
LVHW081317060526
838201LV00055B/2326